ROSE BUSH

LEARN HOW TO GROW A ROSE BUSH FROM A BUD, BLOOM AND BEYOND

By Beverly Hill

D1602292

Introduction

I want to thank you and congratulate you for choosing the book, *"ROSE BUSH: LEARN HOW TO GROW A ROSE BUSH FROM A BUD, BLOOM OR BEYOND"*.

This book contains proven steps and strategies on how to grow various types of roses and how to maintain their bushes.

By all accounts, the rose is without a doubt one of the most beautiful, and most popular flowers in the garden. Not only have roses been around for thousands of years, but they are also relatively easy to grow, and they are grown in virtually all countries. In fact, even if you only have minimal gardening experience you can still grow beautiful roses providing you have at least some understanding with regards to caring for them.

For many years, lovers have given roses, and poets have written of their merits. Now, you may be considering showing how much you love roses by planting your own rose bushes. No doubt you've heard a lot about how to take care of roses- the diseases to watch out for, and the ways to prune them. While it may sound pretty complicated, you'll find that planting your own rose bush is much easier than you think. If you take the following guidelines that are presented in this book into consideration, and use them, you'll be sure to do a great job, and have a beautiful rose bush that will look wonderful.

Thanks again for choosing this book, I hope you enjoy it!

ABOUT THE AUTHOR

Beverly Hill is a sociologist. She is the CEO of C.E.F Associates and formerly served as head of department of sociology in Premier Natural Resources Inc.

A graduate of Nelson High School also graduated from the University of Toronto with a B.A in economics and finance and holds an M.S from Cambridge University in public relations and PhD in sociology.

She has written many articles on human equality, animal rights, environmental issues, personal development and peace keeping in different newspapers. She has also appeared in many magazines and is frequently interviewed for articles on family, race, socioeconomic status, and how to survive in your environment. She has also worked on the importance of health of relationship between parents and children. Her book 'The Middle Child' focuses on the importance of the attention given to the children and what to expect from them. This book helps parents understand their children.

In addition to these works she is also the author of 'Surviving Alone ' which is about her own childhood growing up; she writes about her family struggles living on a low income budget and growing her own food to survive.

C.E.F Associates formed in 1999 in Idaho, USA she worked both nationally and internationally. This is a consulting company which has clients all over the world. Ms. Hill the CEO of the company is the main reason of the huge client base because of her servings in foreign countries.

TABLE OF CONTENT

Chapter 1

THINGS TO DO BEFORE PLANTING YOUR ROSE BUSH

If you are waiting for spring to arrive so you can plant your rose bush, there are some things that you may want to do. You may want to start thinking about the types of bushes you want for your rose garden. There are hundreds of different rose bushes that you can choose from, and it may be a bit difficult to make your choice. You may want to visit a nursery in your area to find out more about bushes. Also, look for friends and neighbors that have beautiful bushes, and find out what types of bushes they are growing. Make sure that you know whether a certain bush is prone to disease, or if it takes a lot of attention as well before making your choice.

Of course once you know what bush you want for your garden, then you'll need to come up with a great location for it as well. Make sure you come up with a good location before you even buy your rose bush. You need to be sure that your bush will get plenty of light each day, and you should make sure that the soil drains well, and that it is quite fertile.

WHEN TO PLANT A ROSE BUSH

Usually, if you are planting a rose bush that is bare root, you will want to plant it late in the winter. However, if you purchase a rose bush that has already been grown in a planter, you'll want to plant it during the spring. Just make sure that you don't plant roses during the summer months. While it is possible, it can be very hard on the new plant because of the hot weather.

Chapter 2

PREPARATION FOR PLANTING YOUR ROSE BUSH

Now that you know what location you're going to plant the rose in, you need to get the bed ready. Make sure that you dig a hole that is going to be at least two times the size of the container holding your rose bush. Remember, the bush has a very large root system. If you make sure that your hole is large, it will be easier for the rose bush to put down its roots.

When you dig out the soil, make sure to put it in a bucket or wheelbarrow. Then mix compost and topsoil with the soil, and put part of the mixture into the hole. In some cases you may want to add phosphate fertilizer in the hole as well.

When you are dealing with a bare root rose bush, you'll want to soak it for awhile before you plant it. Once you have soaked the bush for a least a couple hours, you'll want to cut off the root tips with pruning shears, and then you'll be ready to plant the bush.

PLANTING THE BUSH

There are many bushes that will come along with planting instructions. Usually you'll want to put a mound at the bottom of the hole you have, and then you put the bare root rose bush over this mound, making sure the roots are smoothly placed over it. If your roots curve up or they spread out in a flat manner, then you may not have to use the ground. Then you can start filling the hole back in; however, once you have it about 2/3 full with soil, make sure to water it. Once you have let the whole drain, then fill it again with water, and then add the rest of the soil to the hole.

Chapter 3

CARING FOR YOUR ROSE BUSH

Usually you'll need to give your new rose bush about an inch of water each week, but this can depend on the climate you are living in. Make sure that you recognize when your rose is in distress. If you notice that the leaves are drooping, you'll need to add some water. However, if the leaves are falling off and turning yellow, you may be giving them too much water.

Growing and caring for rose bushes is part of garden maintenances. That's if you have some bushes on your garden areas. Rose bushes are always as beautiful as ever. Just like the human skin, to maintain its glow and beauty, proper caring should be given to them. Roses are the undisputed flowers of most gardeners. Despite the extra care needed to grow the rose bushes in the garden, gardeners and flowers lovers would never mind doing it. It's because roses truly beautifies the garden, and give that feeling of peace, sweetness, and happiness.

Growing and caring for rose bushes is very rewarding and easy especially if you are inclined with flower growing. To get started, you need to have a little knowledge of gardening basics, and a garden location where there is enough sunlight. As you learn all the basics and tips of rose bushes caring, you can turn your garden into a perfect bush of rose profusion. You also need to know more about the particular roses that you are about to grow and care for, so it would be a success for you in creating your own wonderful garden of rose bushes.

Growing and caring for rose bushes can be an invigorating experience. If you decided to this, you need to know the tasks of spraying, fertilizing, and timely pruning of rose plants. You also need to know about the pests and diseases that may damage your rose bushes if not properly taken care of. In taking care of the rose bushes, you need to have the right amount of water for the maintenance and daily care. Once the rose bushes are filled with water, or watered insufficiently, they will die because rose plants are very delicate when it comes to watering.

If the rose bushes experienced too much water, its roots get shallow. If this happens the roots will be unable to absorb vital nutrients, which will help develop the strong root system of the rose plants. Fungal growth is also encouraged once shallow watering happens on the rose bushes. Deep watering is preferred for rose bushes. The leaves of the rose plants are needed to be kept dry to avoid plaguing of diseases. Making the soil around the rose plants to be rich in potassium is also part of caring for rose bushes especially during the flowering season.

Some rose experts suggested that placing some banana peels around the soil of the rose plants, or at the base of the plants would be best, since banana peels are said to be rich in magnesium, potassium, sulfur, and phosphates. This process is also best during the fertilizing season of the rose plants, which is essential for flowering. The pH level of the soil for rose bushes should be maintained between 6.0-6.5. It is recommended to have a regular check on the pH level as well.

Chapter 4

THE PERFECT WAY TO PLANT THE PERFECT ROSE BUSH

Growing roses isn't nearly as hard as most people think it is, but it does require a certain level of knowledge, and a green thumb to grow beautiful roses. Here is information that will help you to plant the perfect rose bush, in the perfect way, so that you, your family, and your neighbors can enjoy beautiful roses in your perfect rose garden for many years to come.

When you purchase a rose bush, you will notice that the roots of the bush are wrapped in moss. Moss usually has a very cool feel to it, and this is important for the survival of your rose bush. The moss should continue to cover the roots until you are ready to plant the bush in your garden. Do not leave the unplanted bush in the sun! It needs a cool place, but that it doesn't have to be extremely cold. An air conditioned house is good, and a nice cool basement is even better.

You will want to get your rose bush planted in the garden as soon as it is possible, as this increases the bushes chances of survival. The planting must take place before spring, which should be possible since the bushes are typically sold towards the end of winter. You will need to refer to zoning charts to determine when the right time to plant your rose bush in the garden of the area that you reside in. In most areas, March is the appropriate month for planting rose bushes. However, in some areas, you will need to wait until April.

Before you plot the rose bush in the ground you will want to carefully consider the location in your garden that you have selected. Rose bushes typically need at least six hours of good sunlight per day. You will need to watch how the sun hits your garden for a least one day, and possibly two or more to get a good read of the sunniest locations in your yard, without subjecting your rose bushes to an over abundance of harsh sunlight.

The area that you select must also drain well. Your rose bush will die if the water on, or in the soil stands for any length of time without draining. This can usually be tended to by placing drain pipes that run off to another location either on top of the soil, or just under the soil with an opening where the water tends to collect. You might also want to create a small mound of soil, so that your rose bush kind of sit up on its own miniature hill within your garden.

Do you have the proper soil for rose bush? If not, this can usually be corrected with soil that you purchase. The soil should have a pH Balance of acid in the range of 5.8 to 6.3. You may need to add lime to your soil to increase the acid. Some people also have luck increasing the acidity of the soil by using pine needles in the soil. Never just assume that your soil is fine because your neighbors have rose bushes in their garden! Your soil could be very different, and they may have treated their soil for the purpose of planting roses.

Rose bushes should be planted at least two feet apart. Many people think that this space refers to the space between the bases of the bushes-where they come out of the ground. While this works, your rose bushes will live more happily in your garden with a bit more space. Try to estimate how far out the branches of the bush will extend, and allow two feet between the bushes from there.

Chapter 5

5 TIPS TO GROW HEALTHY ROSES

Summer is coming, and there's nothing more beautiful than a rose bush covered with lunch blossoms and healthy green leaves. How to grow roses without a lot of strain and effort? Follow these 5 tips and you can grow healthy roses.

PREPARING THE SOIL

If you're planting a rose bush dig a hole about 1/2 times as deep as the rose bush container and twice as wide. Add slow release fertilizer per package directions to the bottom of the hole, then a shovel full of compost, a shovel of the soil you removed, and a bit more fertilizer. Remove the rose bush gently from the container, and set in the hole. The soil line on the rose bush from the container should be the same as in your garden. If it's too high remove a bit more soil from the planting hole. If it's a bit too low add another shovel of soil. When it's just right, gently scratch the roots from the bottom of the root ball and around the sides. That will encourage the roots to start branching out into the new hole.

Fill the hole half way, alternating soil and compost with a sprinkle of fertilizer. Water thoroughly. When the water has been absorbed by the soil, fill the hole to the top, and water again.

REFRESH THE SOIL

Dig a few inches deep around the base of your rose out to the edges of the bush. Remove about half of the soil, and replace with compost, or bagged topsoil, mixed with slow release fertilizer-follow package directions. Add a layer of mulch a couple of inches deep to retain the moisture in the soil. The mulch will break down over the season, and add organic matter to the soil.

CATCH PROBLEMS BEFORE THEY START

If you see aphids, or other buggy creatures remove them immediately. Don't wait until you get to the nursery for bug spray. Most creatures can be washed off with a strong spray of water. Aphids can be sprayed with a mixture of ½ teaspoon dishwashing liquid to one quart of water. Spray on the aphids. If you don't have a sprayer handy use a sponge. It's messier but it works.

Look at your roses as they grow, and treat problems right away. Look at the leaves for disease, or brown spots. Don't get too worried if leaves are a bit yellowish-greenish, or new growth is kind of reddish, that can be normal. If the veins of the leaves are dark green, but the leaf itself is yellow it could be a sign of iron deficiency. That's easily treatable. If the entire leaf is yellow that could be a sign of nitrogen deficiency, again easily corrected.

DON'T OVER WATER

Roses don't like getting their leaves wet, and they don't like keeping their feet wet. Don't water on a preset schedule. Water when the top 3 or 4 inches of soil is dry, and then soak the plants. In very humid climates don't crowd your roses with other plants, it invites fungus diseases. In hot dry climates don't water every day, plant the roses so they receive afternoon shade.

REMOVE SPENT BLOSSOMS

The only purpose of a flower is to produce seed, well at least to the plant that's the only purpose. Remove the spent blossoms, and the rose will continue to bud and flower. The exception is if the rose is of a variety that only blooms once a year. In that case leave the blossoms and enjoy the display.

Follow these easy tips, and you'll have no problems growing healthy roses.

Chapter 6

EVERYTHING ABOUT ROSE BUSH CARE

You'd be hard pressed to find a gardener who has included rose bushes in their floral repertoire, and didn't walk away thrilled with the return on investment received for their efforts. Few garden icons compare to the rose in charm and richness. Grown for thousands of years in almost every corner of the inhabited world, roses have long been considered a symbol of elegance. With some basic knowledge of rose bush care, even beginning gardeners can reap the benefits that all successful rose growers have come to know. Whether you've inherited your rose bushes by moving into a home with an existing garden, or have just planted your first variety, understanding proper rose bush care is simple and rewarding.

There are so many different varieties of rose bushes; your biggest obstacle may be choosing which one is best for you, your color, size, shape, you name it, and you'll find a rose to fit it-and you'll probably really enjoy yourself in the process. Roses fare best when they're planted in good soil, in a sunny spot where they are assured of getting at least six hours of direct sunlight every day.

Those varieties of rose bushes that are said to do well in shade still need four to six hours of direct sunlight daily. Deep watering, about one inch per week, is critical in keeping your rose bushes healthy. The root systems of roses grow deep, and so must the water you give them. Surface watering will not do any good, since there is no way for the roots to extract water at ground level.

Rose bushes are vulnerable to many different kinds of damaging insects like mites, caterpillars, Japanese beetles, and aphids to name just a few. There are several options available to gardeners when it comes to pest control, and the more you learn about each method, the better equipped you will be to handle it with ease. First, identify the invader. If there is one or two wandering the plant, pick them off with your fingers. There is a chance that eggs have been laid on the plant's leaves, so remove the leaf on which you saw the insect to be safe. You can choose between man-made, and organic pest control methods, but it makes sense to learn what you can about both options before making a choice.

Be hyper-vigilant when reading over the labels of any pest control chemical you purchase, since even some organic remedies can be toxic to people, pets, and local wildlife. Carefully follow the package directions whenever using these types of chemicals. Most experienced rose bush growers believe that infestations can be remedied naturally without any chemicals at all.

The pests that attack your roses have their own enemies in nature. Ladybugs, for instance, eat many of the insects that plague roses. Frogs, lizards, snakes, and even certain species of wasps are nature's way of keeping harmful pest off of your rose bushes. Deadheading, or pruning, is another important part of rose bush care. Deadheading your blooms after they fade makes room for a new bud to flower, which will keep your rose bushes vibrant all through the season. Pruning also rids your rose bushes of dead twigs, and other garbage vegetation that will only stunt your rose bush's flowering and growth.

Conclusion

Thank you again for choosing this book!

I hope this book was able to help you to create the perfect rose bush.

Considering the beauty of roses, it's hardly surprising that so many gardeners feel that a garden is incomplete if it has no roses growing in it. Those rose bushes which are properly cared for will boom profusely from June all the way through to the arrival of frost. With just a minimal amount of care, rose bushes can lead your garden a touch of elegance and beauty in a way that no other flower can.

Finally, if you enjoyed this book, would you be kind enough to leave a review for this book on Amazon? It'd be greatly appreciated!

Thank you and good luck!

Preview Of 'GREENHOUSE: HOW TO BUILD YOUR OWN GREENHOUSE' Chapter 1

WHAT IS A GREENHOUSE

The definition of a greenhouse also referred to as a glasshouse sometimes when you have enough heating it is also called a hot house. It's a structure made of walls and roof which is designed or built with transparent materials like glass, and in this structure we have plants (not just any plants but plants requiring controlled climatic conditions) grown within such structure, hence the name Greenhouse is derived from this kind of setting.

The environmental benefits of having a greenhouse is so immense, because of the alarming environmental situation of the world today, especially the problem of global warming, air pollution and all manner of pollution experienced in the environment which we live it really warrants us to start thinking about having a greenhouse. To have a greenhouse is not difficult as some people many think. The materials range in size from small or medium size sheds to much more industrial bigger sized building materials.

GREENHOUSE

HOW TO BUILD YOUR OWN GREENHOUSE

BEVERLY HILL

To check out the rest of (GREENHOUSE: HOW TO BUILD YOUR OWN GREENHOUSE) on Amazon.com

Check Out My Other Books

Below you'll find some of my other popular books that are popular on Amazon and Kindle as well. Alternatively, you can visit my author page on Amazon to see other work done by me.

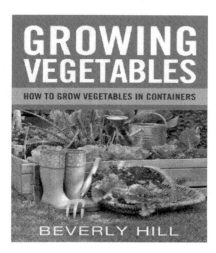

GROWING VEGETABLES: HOW TO GROW VEGETABLES IN CONTAINERS.

COMPANION PLANTING FOR BEGINNERS: LEARN WHICH PLANTS GOES WELL WITH EACH OTHER.

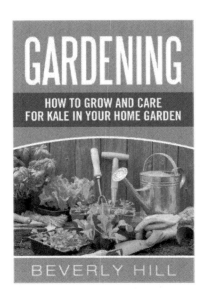

GARDENING: HOW TO GROW AND CARE FOR KALE IN YOUR HOME GARDEN.

GREENHOUSE GROWING FOR BEGINNERS: HOW TO GROW VEGETABLES AND FLOWERS.

GREENHOUSE GUIDE FOR BEGINNERS: LEARN THE MOST POPULAR VEGETABLES AND FRUITS TO GROW IN A GREENHOUSE.

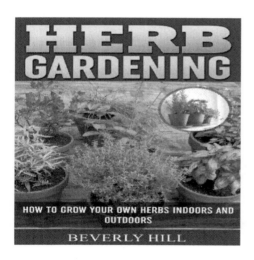

HERB GARDENING: HOW TO GROW YOUR OWN HERBS INDOORS AND OUTDOORS.

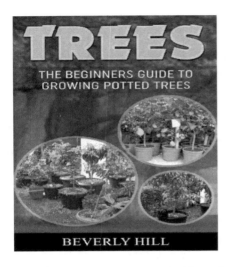

TREES: THE BEGINNERS GUIDE TO GROWING POTTED TREES.

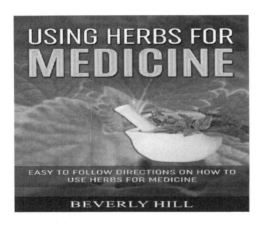

USING HERBS FOR MEDICINE: EASY TO FOLLOW DIRECTIONS ON HOW TO USE HERBS FOR MEDICINE.

You can simply search for these titles on the Amazon website to find them.

BONUS: SUBSCRIBE TO THE FREE BOOK

Beginners Guide to Yoga & Meditation

"Stressed out? Do You Feel Like The World Is Crashing Down Around You? Want To Take A Vacation That Will Relax Your Mind, Body And Spirit? Well this Easy To Read Step By Step

E-Book Makes It All Possible!"

Instructions on how to join our mailing list, and receive a free copy of "Yoga and Meditation" can be found in any of my Kindle eBooks.

NOTES

NOTES

NOTES

NOTES

NOTES

Made in the USA
San Bernardino, CA
28 March 2019